W9-BEB-191

LifeCaps Presents:

Dido Elizabeth Belle:

A Biography

By Fergus Mason

BookCaps™ Study Guides
www.bookcaps.com

© 2014. All Rights Reserved.

Table of Contents

About LifeCaps

LifeCaps is an imprint of BookCaps™ Study Guides. With each book, a lesser known or sometimes forgotten life is recapped. We publish a wide array of topics (from baseball and music to literature and philosophy), so check our growing catalogue regularly (**www.bookcaps.com**) to see our newest books.

Introduction

Imagine an upper-class English family around the time of the American Revolution. They would be wealthy, living in a big house run by dozens of servants. They'd be well dressed in elaborate fashions, often embellished with fabrics and jewels imported from Britain's growing overseas possessions. They might be politically influential; members of the family could be prominent in the legal profession or hold high ranks in the military. They would have extensive business interests both in Britain and abroad. And, of course, they'd be white.

Today, the United Kingdom is a diverse nation. Twelve per cent of the population is non-white, with the majority of those being British-born. Black and Asian Britons can be found at high levels in the government, in the arts, in sport and in academia. The House of Lords is ethnically mixed, as are the Queen's guards. In 1780 it was very different Out of a British population of about 7.5 million less than 25,000 – a third of a per cent – were non-white, and a significant proportion of those were slaves. There were a handful of successful and well-known black writers, actors and musicians, but the country was to all intents and purposes racially homogenous.

Then, as now, London was a large and populous city – one in seven of the entire British population lived there. Even in the 18th century much of the city was densely built up, packed with houses and businesses, but there were also plenty of green open areas. One of the largest is Hampstead Heath, 800 acres of grassland and woods at the northern edge of London. The Heath itself is common land, a popular place for Londoners to walk and relax, but around it are several big houses – the residences of the rich and famous. One of the grandest of those is Kenwood House, and in 1780 it was the residence of England's most senior judge.

Imagine the scene inside Kenwood House. Despite the lack of electricity it was a place of incredible luxury, with an interior designed by one of the best architects of the time and furnished with no regard for expense. There were over fifty rooms, all kept in order by a large staff of servants. The library was one of the finest in the country. When the Lord Chief Justice wasn't in court or at his town house this was a place where he could relax, walk in the grounds or work on his case notes. He shared it with his wife and their two adopted daughters, who in fact were his great-nieces – the children of two of his nephews, placed in his care because they had both lost their mothers. These two girls enjoyed good educations, the finest clothes and a fabulously wealthy, privileged lifestyle. They were Elizabeth Murray and Dido Elizabeth Belle, and the Mansfields pampered them as if they were their own children. Of course many people were bringing up the children of relatives – death in childbirth was a common event. The family at Kenwood was remarkable, though. Dido Elizabeth Belle, foster child of an Earl and natural daughter of a Royal Navy admiral, was black.

Chapter 1: War in the New World

The first surprising thing about the Seven Years War is that it lasted for nine years. It could also be classed as the first global war, because it was fought on six continents and involved every one of the major European imperial powers plus a host of allies. The main conflict was between Britain on one side and France on the other and, as with so many 18th and 19th century wars, the issue in dispute was trade. Other nations and empires joined the war in the hope of getting some advantage from supporting one of the superpowers. The Protestant northern German states sided with Britain to gain a backer against Catholic Austria, which favored France and Spain. Portugal also joined the British side in the hope of rebuilding the eminence it had lost to Spain. Other decaying empires, like Sweden and the India-based Mughals, hoped France could roll back the growing power of British merchants and the Redcoats who cleared the way for them.

In the USA the Seven Years War is usually called the French and Indian War; the fighting on land, which took place from 1754 to 1763, was mostly between the colonists of New France on one side and the British colonists on the other. The French were badly outnumbered but managed to persuade several Native American tribes to join them. On the other hand the British were supported by the powerful Iroquois Confederation. Battles rolled back and forth across Canada and what's now the southeastern USA for several years, with the French looking like winning in the summer of 1757; the year went so badly for Britain that the government fell. The new Prime Minister was William Pitt the elder, and he reorganized the military leadership in North America and sent fresh troops across the Atlantic. In 1758 the vengeful British surged out from behind their defenses and began rolling up their enemies. By 1760 fighting on the North American mainland was almost over. Then, in 1762, Spain entered the war on the French side.

France had been the most dangerous enemy of England, and later Great Britain, since the early 14th century and the two nations had often clashed on land. At sea, however, France was a minor player and the only nation that could defeat the growing power of the Royal Navy was Spain. The Spanish had built a huge fleet to support (and bring gold from) their colonies in South and Central America, and for centuries their huge, heavily armed galleons were the masters of the sea. In the religious wars that constantly ravaged Europe the riches of the New World gave Spain enormous power and the English had put a lot of effort into disrupting that trade. In an early example of asymmetric warfare they had licensed privateers to prey on the treasure galleons. Out at sea the big ships were safe from anything but a storm, but primitive navigation and ocean weather patterns forced a fatal flaw into their sailing plans. Sailing directly to Spain from the treasure ports of South America meant fighting against the northeasterly trade winds all the way home, which could add weeks to the voyage and even endanger the ship. Instead they sailed up the coast and across the Caribbean, sailed out to Bermuda – which was used for centuries as a waypoint, and is surrounded by wrecks as a result – then turned east and struck out across the ocean, following the westerly trade winds back to Europe. If, of course, they made it that far.

For 1,400 miles, from Port of Spain in Venezuela to New Providence in the Bahamas, the route of the Spanish ships took them through the islands of the West Indies. That was where small ships packed with desperate men – privateers when England and Spain were at war, simple pirates the rest of the time – could close on a galleon during the night and overwhelm its crew. Tens of millions of Spanish dollars, gold and silver worth billions at today's prices, was looted from ships and ports by the buccaneers. In an effort to protect the treasure ships the Spanish built powerful naval bases on their possessions in the Caribbean, with the biggest of them located at Havana. The British, determined to expand their colonies and influence in North America, wanted the Spanish bases out. Now, with Spain's declaration of war, they had an excuse to move against them.

Havana, July 1762

Captain John Lindsay was doing well out of this war. He'd joined the Royal Navy in 1753, then three years later passed his exams to be commissioned as a Lieutenant and was lucky enough to be given an independent command straight away. It was only a fireship, the *Pluto*; a small, elderly merchantman loaded with flammable material and intended to be set ablaze and left to drift into an enemy harbor, but for an ambitious young officer it was an opportunity. Until the day he ignited his ship and took to the boats with is crew he would be sailing her in company with a fleet, and if he did a good job of it that would be noticed. It was; in 1757 he was promoted and put in command of the newly built frigate HMS *Trent*.[i]

Most of the firepower of an 18th century navy was concentrated in ships of the line – huge, slab-sided floating fortresses with two or even three decks carrying anywhere between 60 and 100 heavy guns. In battle the opposing fleets would form into lines, which would close in and pound each other with their cannons until one side had had enough. The massive ships were key to winning sea battles, but they were also expensive and needed huge crews to man their guns – and trained seamen were always in short supply. They couldn't be spared for other tasks, like escorting convoys or patrolling in search of the enemy, so they were supplemented with large numbers of smaller ships. The most important of these were frigates.

Frigates were usually almost as long as ships of the line, and carried similar sails, but they only had a single gun deck so their hulls were lower and lighter. That made them faster and more agile, so they were ideal for scouting or raiding. Because they were frequently sent away from the fleet frigate commanders had a lot of independence and it was a highly prized job; to be given one only a year after being commissioned shows that Lindsay was well thought of by his superiors. Of course as a junior officer he hadn't been given the best frigate in the fleet. HMS *Trent* was brand new, one of the successful 28-gun *Coventry* class, but to get as many ships in service as quickly as possible she and four others of the class had been built of fir instead of the traditional oak. Fir was cheaper and easier to work with, but it rotted quickly – on average these ships only lasted nine years before being scrapped. HMS *Trent* was launched in 1757 and by 1764 she was being broken up in a salvage yard, her timbers riddled with shipworms and tropical rot. For the first few years of the war, however, she was an active part of the British fleet. When Lindsay first took command he patrolled the waters around the British Isles to guard against French raiders, then transferred to the West Indies squadron under Sir George Pocock. In May 1762 his ship joined an amphibious assault force of 23 line of battle ships, eleven frigates, eight smaller warships and nearly 13,000 soldiers; their target was Havana.

Havana had one of the best harbors in the West Indies, secure against storms and with enough space for over a hundred large ships. Access was through a channel nearly a mile long and only 200 yards wide, which could be blocked by a heavy chain that stretched across the entrance. Two fortresses, Morro Castle and San Salvador de la Punta, protected the channel; even with the chain lowered to the seabed any ship trying to get through would be battered by the heavy guns that bristled from the ramparts; Morro Castle had 64 guns and San Salvador around 20, and between 30 and 40 of those guns could be fired into the channel. Fortress guns were particularly feared by the Royal Navy because the Spanish were pioneers in the use of heated shot; the iron cannonballs would be loaded into a furnace until they were red hot, then taken to the guns. The artillerymen had to aim and fire quickly before the glowing metal burned through the soaked wadding and detonated the charge, but the effects could be devastating. A 64 pound ball of red hot iron, embedded in the shattered timbers of the target, would quickly start a huge fire. On a sailing battleship, an inflammable mass of painted wood, tarred rope and sailcloth with a hundred tons of gunpowder in its magazines, fire would be a disaster. The British knew they had to capture the forts before they could get access to the harbor and wipe out the Spanish force there.

The Spanish fleet was strong too; they had nine ships of the line, 9,000 soldiers, the artillerymen in the forts and about 2,800 local militia. They didn't have enough naval power to beat the British in a straight-up fight, but nine battleships was enough to seriously threaten British convoys throughout the Caribbean or hammer towns along the coasts; if Havana wasn't captured and the ships seized or destroyed the Royal Navy would have to keep a powerful force of its own off Havana to bottle them up, and with the hurricane season approaching they didn't want to do that. Instead they planned to land troops, besiege the Morro Castle, breach its walls with artillery and capture it. That, they hoped, would force the Spaniards to surrender.

The British were experts at siege warfare but they were used to doing it in Europe, where trenches could be easily dug. When the first troops landed on the north side of the harbor entrance they found the ground was too rocky for their tools. Normally they would have dug trenches towards the fortress, sheltering in them to avoid fire from the walls. Gun batteries would be excavated so the siege artillery could batter the walls and the trenches themselves would be pushed as close to the defenses as possible, allowing the attackers to stay under cover until the last moments when they rushed towards the breach. Faced with the rocky ground they had to find an alternative. Luckily, they did. The Morro Castle was built right on the edge of the channel and there was higher ground behind it – a low hill called La Cabana. It wasn't much higher, only 23 feet above the walls, but that was enough. Guns on La Cabana would be able to fire over the outer defenses and hit the walls. By June 22 the British had landed twelve heavy siege guns and were slamming balls into the walls of the fortress, gradually breaking up the stonework. At the same time more than three dozen mortars dropped explosive shells into the fort, killing men, burning supplies and dismounting guns. Meanwhile the troops worked their way forwards. They couldn't dig trenches but a Royal Engineers officer came up with the idea of using breastworks – rough walls of earth, brushwood and stone. The troops, sweating in blazing sunshine, slowly built up the crude ramparts and extended them forwards under the fire of the Spanish defenders.

As June went on the fire from the walls dwindled; every day more guns were smashed and more infantry cut down by the mortar shells. The Spanish tried to destroy the gun batteries on June 29, sending a thousand men to attack the besiegers, but the British threw them back and the guns kept firing.

The siege was going too slowly, though, and the British were in a hurry. The Spanish and French weren't their only enemies; they also faced the ravages of yellow fever. Transmitted by the bite of mosquitos, this disease is a deadly menace in the tropical and subtropical areas of South America and Africa. Even today, with an effective vaccine in use, it's very difficult to treat; 200,000 people a year catch the disease, mostly in Africa where vaccination is less common, and one in seven of them die. In the 18th century there was no vaccine and treatment was far more primitive, so the disease could devastate military units or ships' crews. With men crammed closely together in ships or camps mosquitos would move between the sick and the healthy, carrying the deadly virus with them. The infection was rife on Cuba and it quickly gained a foothold in the British encampments, By late June half their men were sick or already dead and they were worried that by the time the guns brought the wall down they wouldn't have enough men to storm the fortress. As the month turned they attempted to hurry things up.

On July 1 Admiral Pocock sent four of his battleships into the channel mouth to bombard the remaining guns on the fortress walls. At the same time the siege batteries fired faster than ever as the gunners sweated frantically at the huge cannons. It was an ambitious plan and it was only a partial success. The artillerymen pounded the landward side of the fort, and by sunset only three guns remained on that wall. The ships were mercilessly battered, though. The fort was too high above the channel for their guns to hit the Spanish cannons; the balls slammed harmlessly into the thick stonework that protected the guns. At the same time fire from both forts pounded the attackers. Nearly 200 men were killed and three of the ships were seriously damaged – HMS *Stirling Castle* was so mauled that after the battle she was stripped of useful equipment and deliberately sunk, while HMS *Marlborough* and HMS ran into bad weather on the way home from England and her crew had to be taken off the leaking hulk. Meanwhile on HMS *Cambridge* her commander, Captain William Goostrey, was killed by a ball from a Spanish musket.

John Lindsay was cruising not far offshore in HMS *Trent*. Frigates were often used as a screening force – their speed made them ideal for spotting any approaching enemy. Their guns only fired 12-pound shot, however, compared to the massive 24 and 32-pounders carried by ships of the line, and their timbers were much lighter than the big ships; they needed to stay well clear of an alerted enemy fortress. That's just what Lindsay was doing, until he saw that *Cambridge* was in trouble. The Spanish fire had killed two dozen men on the battleship and wounded nearly a hundred more, and a disproportionate number of the casualties were officers – they were exposed on deck while most of the crew were below with the guns and protected behind over a foot of solid oak, which would stop anything short of heavy cannonballs. Now the 80-gun ship was caught in the crossfire from the two forts and her crew was effectively leaderless – none of the surviving officers had the experience to get her out. A signal flag was hoisted to show the captain as dead, and it was seen on *Trent*. Lindsay ordered his own crew to take *Trent* inshore, close enough for him to be rowed to the *Cambridge* in one of his ship's boats. Then he climbed aboard the bigger ship, took command and brought her safely out. His actions were noticed by the admiral and gave his reputation a massive boost.

The naval attack had failed, but the British were still in a hurry. Now they came up with a new plan – extend their breastworks to a point where they could dig a ditch right up to the fort, then place a huge mine. Unfortunately there was a delay – on July 2 the muzzle blast of the guns set fire to the wooden supports of the breastworks that surrounded the artillery positions, and the blaze destroyed the battery. The Spanish used the lull in the shelling to patch the worst of the damage to the wall and repair many of their guns, but cannon were brought from the warships to replace the burned siege artillery and new batteries were built. By July 17 the Morro Castle had only two guns left and the British began digging towards the walls. The Spanish could see something was happening and launched raids by land and sea to disrupt the work, but they failed. By July 29 the diggers had reached the fort and barrels of gunpowder were brought forward.

The landward wall of the Morro Castle was protected by a deep ditch that could be swept by fire from projecting bastions at each corner, but the Spanish guns had been destroyed and the heavy shelling had forced them to pull their men off the fort's ramparts. The British engineers could work safely. Now they dug into the inner face of the ditch and stacked their powder barrels.

Storming a fortress was bloody, vicious work. If the defenders held firm the attackers were often shot to pieces as they tried to climb the breach; if the assault succeeded against fierce opposition the enraged troops often massacred the surviving defenders. The British hoped the Spanish could be persuaded to surrender and launched a fake attack as a show of force, but the fort's commander was unmoved. In fact next day two small ships landed a raiding party in an attempt to destroy the mine. The British had had enough; they lit the fuse. At 1:00pm on July 30 the explosives packed into the face of the ditch went off with a deafening roar. The blast ripped out a length of the wall's foundations and sent cracks through the stonework above. Pulled down by its own weight a huge chunk of the bastion's face crumbled and collapsed into the ditch. The rubble formed a rough ramp leading from the floor of the ditch up through the shattered wall and into the fortress. The dust had barely settled when seven hundred picked redcoats came out of the swirling powder smoke and started clawing their way up the ramp. The commander of the fort rushed to the breach with a group of men but by the time they got there the leading redcoats had already secured the top of the breach. The fighting inside was hand to hand, and it was brutal but short. The commander, Luis Vicente de Velasco, was cut down by a musket ball and as the British spread out into the fort with levelled bayonets his men began to surrender. They yielded quickly enough to save their lives; the redcoats hadn't had to fight through the slaughter of a defended breach, so tempers were relatively calm. The dying Velasco was sent to Havana under a white flag along with an offer of surrender terms.

Havana itself was commanded by the Captain General of Cuba, Juan de Prado. An aristocrat and professional soldier, he was not the most competent of men. He was also worried. When he'd arrived in Havana in 1761 one of his orders from the King of Spain had been to fortify the La Cabana hill and strengthen the Morro Castle against a British attack, and he hadn't done it. It wasn't entirely his fault, because a yellow fever outbreak had decimated his workforce, but he could still have done more to protect the city and now it was in grave danger. On July 31 Velasco died and a truce was arranged for his funeral, but meantime the British were building a line of new gun batteries along the north side of the channel. Fresh siege artillery and more heavy guns landed from the ships were being lined up in the positions, their muzzles pointing at the La Punta fort and the city itself. Havana was one of the richest cities in the New World and a huge prize for the British. As well as the ships trapped in the harbor there were two more partly built ships of the line in the shipyards, large reserves of silver and gold and warehouses crammed with trade goods. There were also tens of thousands of slaves.

Chapter 2: The Shameful Trade - Slavery

Slavery in Cuba reached its height long after the attack of 1762; in fact the British shipped in 5,000 slaves during their occupation of Havana and that encouraged landowners to rely more on captive labor after the island returned to Spanish control. There were already many sugar plantations in Cuba when the redcoats landed, though, and without modern technology sugar farming relied on slaves to do the back-breaking work of cutting then crushing the tough stalks. The black population of Cuba in 1762 was a curious mixture. Most were slaves, but a large number were semi-free. Free blacks weren't allowed to live in the white-only city of Havana[ii] but otherwise they could live, work and trade more or less as they pleased. Many of them were fiercely loyal to Spain and joined the local militia which helped defend the city; incredibly many of the slaves were just as loyal. It didn't hurt that when the British approached Captain General Prado announced that any slave who volunteered for the militia would be freed.[iii] Many accepted his offer and they fought bravely and well during the siege.

Slavery has existed since at least the beginning of recorded history. The Babylonians, Egyptians, Greeks and Romans enslaved prisoners of war or conquered peoples; the Bible gives instructions on how to buy or sell slaves and orders slaves to work hard for Christian owners. Raiding Norsemen carried away women and children to use as labor on their Scandinavian farms or for sale in the busy slave markets of the Byzantine Empire and the Middle East. Ideas about human rights were very different – almost nonexistent, in fact – and slavery was an accepted part of life. It slowly began to fade in Europe in the Middle Ages; it was almost extinct in Britain by around 1100, as new farming methods made it uneconomical.[iv] It lasted longer in Eastern Europe and around the Mediterranean; Poland didn't outlaw slavery until the 15th century and in Russia the last slaves were freed (or at least redesignated as serfs, which didn't really improve their lives much) in 1723. Religious orders like the Knights of Malta continued to sell captured enemies into slavery until the 18th century, and the Islamic armies who threatened Europe enslaved millions of people. The Ottoman Empire used galley slaves to power its navy and Muslim pirates from North Africa raided coastal towns as far away as England and Ireland to seize captives. The last slave ports along the North African coast were destroyed by the Royal Navy during the Napoleonic Wars.

Even as slavery faded in Western Europe, though, the expansion of empires gave it a new lease of life in the Americas. Agriculture in Europe was mostly built around large landowners who used tenant farmers as manpower, but the social structure that depended on didn't exist in the New World. Colonists also found themselves with vast areas to farm, often many times greater than they were used to in Europe. Manpower was needed to work on this land, and all too many of them turned to slavery as the answer. The Spanish were the first to ship slaves across the Atlantic, to their colonies in Cuba and Haiti. At first they'd used the native people as slaves but disease had practically wiped them out. The native people of the Americas had almost no resistance to European infections like smallpox, typhus, cholera, mumps or even measles, and died in huge numbers. When Cortez invaded Mexico in 1519 his men brought smallpox with them and within a year half the local population was dead or dying.[v] It wasn't long before the supply of manpower in the New World was essentially wiped out.

The solution was provided by the Portuguese. Their explorers had been working their way down the west coast of Africa building settlements and reported that everywhere north of the Namib Desert was heavily populated. The Portuguese traded with the locals as they went and discovered that there was a thriving slave trade between the various tribes. They quickly joined the trade themselves; colonists began growing sugar on the São Tomé islands in the Gulf of Guinea, and they bought slaves from the mainland tribes to work the fields. It wasn't long before the Spanish joined in, shipping thousands of captives a year to their possessions in South America, Florida and the Caribbean. Soon the other European imperial powers joined in; in the end over ten million people were forcibly transported across the Atlantic, most of them from Togo, Benin, Angola, the Congo, Nigeria and Cameroon. The trade had a huge impact on Africa, as local rulers realized they could obtain fortunes in cash and European products by selling slaves. Wars were fought solely to seize captives, and condemnation to slavery – a traditional punishment for various crimes - skyrocketed. Populations in some parts of West Africa still haven't recovered from these depredations. By the time the British attacked Havana in 1762 Europeans – mostly the French – were bringing over 50,000 slaves a year to the Caribbean.

Several of the European nations – Spain and the Netherlands, for example – had banned slavery at home but tolerated it in their colonies. Britain hadn't outlawed it, but that was mostly because England was one of the first countries where it had died out naturally and it wasn't a big enough issue to be worth passing a law. There were some slaves in Britain but they were few and far between, and tended to be domestic servants rather than farm laborers. The practice existed in a legal gray area; it wasn't forbidden, but it had no support in law either (unless you were a salt factory worker or coal miner in Scotland – until 1799 these luckless tradesmen belonged to the business they worked in and could be sold with it). British planters in the Americas were a very different story, of course; while they didn't import slaves as enthusiastically as the French or Spanish they still had thousands. There was already an active Abolitionist movement in Britain by 1762, and in fact the Lord Chief Justice had ruled in 1701 that a slave became a free man as soon as he arrived in England.[vi] It was a confused situation, and the law wasn't clear. In general slavery was disapproved of in Britain itself but much more widely accepted in the colonies.

The Royal Navy was just as confused on the issue as the rest of Britain. Later it probably played a bigger part than any other organization in ending the slave trade; from 1807 British warships patrolled off the African coast to seize slave ships and free their captives, and some captains even landed heavily armed boarding parties to depose or kill local rulers who refused to stop the trade. In 1762 the situation was more ambiguous. The Navy used slave labor at its dockyards in Jamaica and Antigua, and some senior officers took slaves to sea as personal servants (even though this was against regulations). At the same time the service was always desperate for men and any runaway slave who found his way to a British warship could gain freedom by enlisting as a sailor. Life on an 18th century warship wasn't much easier than life on a sugar plantation but it was adequately paid and the Navy flatly refused to hand runaway slaves back to their owners. There was also the major advantage that on discharge the former slave could settle in Britain or any of her colonies as a free man. It was a similar offer to the one Captain General Prado had made to the slaves of Cuba as the British approached.

Completing their gun batteries took the British ten days after their capture of the Morro Castle, and through that time they kept negotiating with Prado in the hope of persuading him to surrender. They'd been reinforced in mid-July by fresh troops from North America but yellow fever was still cutting away at their strength; they didn't want to lose any more men fighting their way into the city. Prado refused to give up, though, and on July 11 the new batteries opened fire. Their first target was the La Punta fort, and by the end of the day they had battered much of it to rubble and wrecked all its guns. Then they aimed their cannons and mortars at the city itself. Prado had run out of options; if he didn't surrender the guns would open fire again and this time the city itself would be devastated. He sent a messenger to the British telling them he was ready to negotiate.

It took three days to arrange the Spanish surrender but on July 14 redcoats moved into the city and disarmed the defenders. The channel had been blocked with three old ships sunk behind the barrier chain and the navy had to blow them up with gunpowder before they could get any ships in, but that was a priority for them – the admiral commanding the Spanish squadron should have burned his ships to keep them out of the hands of the Royal Navy but he'd failed to do so. Now ten ships of the line – a fifth of Spain's entire fleet of battleships – were British prizes, along with two more almost complete in the dockyards. The Royal Navy would refit the ships and take them into service, giving its forces in the Caribbean a massive boost. Now that Havana had surrendered getting people into the harbor and on board those ships was their top goal. John Lindsay, back in command of HMS *Trent* after his rescue of the stricken HMS *Cambridge*, was one of the officers sent to take control of the Spanish fleet. Many historians believe he found more to look at than captured warships.

Chapter 3: Maria

Captain John Lindsay was a member of the Scottish aristocracy; his father was Sir Alexander Lindsay, 3rd Baronet of Evelix, and as well as carrying British titles the Lindsays were high-ranking members of the Scottish clan system. Sir Alexander died on May 6 1762, so when the Battle of Havana was fought John might not have been told that his older brother was now the 4th Baronet. He himself didn't inherit any title; in 1770 he became Sir John but that was a reward for his performance as a commander, not a family matter. Still, even without a title he was a member of the upper class. That meant there were many social rules he was expected to follow and any indiscretion could cause a major scandal for his family. Something as simple as greeting fellow aristocrats in the wrong order could start people talking about him, and inappropriate contact with a woman of his own class – even going for a walk without a chaperone – could end in disgrace.

It's easy to imagine the horrified reaction of his fellow officers when, sometime within a year before or after the Battle of Havana, he fathered a child with an African slave.

John Lindsay was born in the village of Evelix sometime in 1737. Evelix is hardly bigger today than it was then, just a couple of dozen houses scattered loosely around a junction on the main road to Inverness. A mile and a half to the south lies the Dornoch Firth, a wide river estuary haunted by wading birds. The nearest town with any sort of amenities is the small coast resort of Dornoch, two miles to the west. Evelix itself is too small even to have a pub, the social center of almost every British village. The dwellings are farmhouses and laborer's cottages, many of them ancient structures built from big blocks of gray locally quarried stone. In the 18th century the small farmers would all have been tenants of the Lindsay family. As a Baronet Sir Alexander wasn't a lord and so didn't automatically have a seat in Parliament, but he still ranked above anyone else in the area. The landowning aristocracy mostly lived off rents from their tenants and while that could make a family immensely rich in the green fields of England or the Scottish lowlands, the area around Evelix is a lot tougher. Cold winds from the North Sea constantly sweep the area and the soil is thin and rocky. It's not bad lands by the standards of the Scottish Highlands – most of which can only be used for grazing sheep – but it's not the breadbasket of the nation. Before modern machinery and fertilizers farmers had to work hard to scrape a living from their fields, so it's unlikely the Lindsays earned a fortune in land fees.

In aristocratic families the eldest son would inherit the title and the second would usually join the military. The third, very often, became a clergyman. The Lindsays followed this tradition; David was brought up with an eye on his future duties as the head of the family, while John put on a uniform. Perhaps his choice of service says something about the family's financial situation. In the British Army at the time most officers except technical specialists (the engineers and artillery) purchased their commissions. Promotion by merit was possible, but rare; the usual system was for an officer to buy promotion to the next rank up. The system was widely criticized both within and outside the service, although it wasn't as disastrous as it sounds – officers had to spend at least a certain number of years at one rank before they could purchase a promotion, and the terminally incompetent were usually forced to resign by peer pressure. Commissions were also sold for a particular regiment, and the Colonel could refuse an offer if he didn't like the officer. Nevertheless it was expensive. Each promotion had an official price – for example a Lieutenant had to pay £1,500 (about $330,000 in 2014 dollars) for a Captain's commission – but in practice a place in a fashionable regiment could cost more than twice that.

The Royal Navy, however, didn't use the purchase system. Aspiring officers went to sea as midshipmen, often when they were as young as thirteen, to get practical experience of seamanship. After at least three years, and usually when they were aged 18 or 19, they sat an exam for promotion to Lieutenant. This was a fairly terrifying ordeal; the candidate was grilled by three senior captains, who would rapidly fire questions at him. After that promotion was by seniority and merit. That meant an officer who couldn't afford to buy his way up the ranks could do as well as his richer colleagues, unlike in the army. If the Lindsay family didn't have a huge amount of money to spare the Navy would have been the ideal choice.

There are few records mentioning John Lindsay's early career in the Navy. Many sources say that he joined not long after the Seven Years War broke out, but he was promoted to Lieutenant in 1756 so must have joined in 1753 or earlier. It's known that after being promoted he was given command of a fireship. These didn't rate a senior officer as captain but they, like other small ships, were usually commanded by an experienced Lieutenant; the fact that Lindsay was given his own ship straight away suggests that he had performed well as a midshipman and impressed the examining officers at his exam.

No details of Lindsay's career on the fireship survive; the next record of him is from September 29, 1757, when he was given command of HMS *Trent*.[vii] From a fireship to a frigate would have been an unusually large step, so it's possible that in the meantime the old *Pluto* had been set on fire and launched at some unsuspecting enemy, and Lindsay had moved on to command a brig or cutter. Either way, by late 1757 he was the commander of a real warship and attached to the home fleet. This was a major opportunity. At the time the Royal Navy used the prize system; if an enemy ship was captured it and its contents would either be sold at auction or bought into service by the Navy, and its value would be shared between the admiral commanding the local fleet and the crew of the ship that had captured it. The home fleet spent most of its time blockading the French Atlantic ports, and for the captain of a fast, well-armed frigate there were many opportunities to snap up enemy ships trying to run the blockade. In February 1759 *Trent*, along with HMS *Vestal*, attacked and captured the French frigate *La Bellone* in the English Channel.[viii]

By 1760 *Trent's* budget fir construction was starting to show its drawbacks. Her hull was still reasonably watertight but some of her timbers were riddled with *Teredo navalis*, the naval shipworm. This creature, actually a species of clam, uses the sharp edges of its shell to bore tunnels into wood. It doesn't just use the tunnel as shelter; it actually eats the fragments it scrapes away, so once it's settled on a piece of wood it keeps drilling until the timber has been reduced to a sodden, spongy mass. The navy sheathed the lower hulls of its ships in copper to give some protection, but the covering was never fully sealed and the tiny shipworm larvae would eventually find their way in through gaps and start gouging. Now *Trent* was hauled into the dry dock at Portsmouth, the damaged wood ripped out and replaced, and the whole ship was given a thick coat of varnish. With new copper nailed in place she was loaded with barrels of hard bread, salt beef and fresh water then ordered to cross the Atlantic and join the West Indies squadron. She sailed in late summer and by early November was hard at work hunting down French ships around Martinique. For the next year and a half Lindsay cruised the Caribbean, sometimes working with other frigates and sometimes alone. Then, in May 1762, she joined the fleet preparing for the assault on Havana.

HMS *Trent* returned to England in August 1763 and Lindsay was ordered to prepare her for scrapping; after three years in tropical waters her hull was now a mess. On September 9 he paid off the crew and formally decommissioned the ship.[ix] She was sold at Portsmouth Dockyard on January 26, 1764. She had already been stripped of her guns and all usable military equipment; now her hulk was broken up and the usable timber salvaged. Lindsay, now a well favored commander thanks to his successful time on the frigate, moved on to a new ship.

So when did Lindsay meet Dido's mother? That's the first mystery of her life. All that's known for sure about Dido's mother is that she was an African slave and that her name was probably Maria. Many accounts call her Maria Belle, including the only reference to her in an official British document – her daughter's baptism record. In any case there were many opportunities for Lindsay to meet a slave woman. It's unlikely he did so at any of the British naval bases he would have visited; most of the slaves employed there were men, laborers in the dockyards who helped the shipwrights repair the warships. In any case opportunities for a liaison would have been severely limited. While a ship was in commission her captain was forbidden from spending a night ashore without the permission of the admiral commanding the station and this rule was strictly enforced, especially for frigate commanders. That would have limited his ability to form a relationship with a woman he'd met on shore.

The legend is that Lindsay and Maria met when he rescued her from a Spanish ship, and it's often said that this was one of the ships captured in Havana harbor. That's a definite possibility. The fleet had been stripped of its marines and many sailors, who had been added to the garrisons of the forts and the city, but there were still hundreds of men on each ship; if the Royal Navy had forced its way through the defenses the fleet would have had to be ready to fight. The captains would have remained on board with enough officers and men to work the guns, and that means there were almost certainly slaves on board too.

Conditions on an 18th century sailing ship were harsh. For the sailors they were actively grim; hundreds of men slept in hammocks on the gun decks, only a few inches from the men on either side, with almost no space to store their few belongings. Officers had it slightly better. Most of them had small cabins, and could eat and relax in the wardroom. The captain lived and ate alone in the great cabin at the stern of the ship and had a small bedroom there, too, meaning that he alone had some privacy. He also had servants – at a minimum a steward who looked after his uniform and brought his meals, and usually a clerk to help with the ship's paperwork. Many captains on larger ships also kept additional servants, and these could include women.

Officially no navy allowed women to sail on warships, but in practice it happened all the time.[x] Ships in transit to a new duty station often carried officers' (and even sailors') wives, especially in wartime – they were safer on a warship than on a merchantman that might be captured by an enemy. Some captains had female servants, and even wives or mistresses, living on board. Even the enlisted men on the lower decks were rarely starved of female company. Every time a ship entered port local traders would come out in small craft to make deals with the sailors, who were seldom allowed ashore. They offered food, alcohol – for some sailors their daily ration of a gallon of beer or half a pint of rum just wasn't enough – and prostitutes. A big warship in port would often have hundreds of women on the gundecks, and some stayed on board when the ships went back to sea. The men would hide them from the officers and feed them from their own rations, but in combat the women often helped care for the wounded and sometimes even replaced dead sailors at the guns. Navies knew that, within limits, having women on board could actually reduce discipline problems, so they turned a blind eye. In the Spanish navy - where the officer corps was less professional and more dominated by politically connected aristocrats - there was almost nothing to stop a captain having slaves on board as domestic servants.

So Lindsay could have met Maria after the fall of Havana, either on board one of the captured warships or in the city. He could also have met her earlier, though. Britain had declared war against Spain on January 4, 1762, and as soon as that news reached the Caribbean (it could take over a month) any Spanish ships Lindsay saw would have been fair game. In fact the Royal Navy had already been seizing Spanish ships for some time, if they were caught running the blockades on French-held islands. Lindsay had taken at least two Spanish vessels as prizes in 1761 and Maria could have been on board either of them. She could even have been on a French or Dutch ship – there's no real evidence that she was a captive of the Spanish.

In a year and a half on the West Indies station Lindsay had taken hundreds of prisoners from captured ships. Most of them had been exchanged for British captives in enemy hands, either directly under a flag of truce or by landing them on British islands until an exchange could be negotiated. Military prisoners were detained, and later shipped back to prison camps in England. He had also picked up escaping slaves and set them free in Jamaica and Antigua. If Maria had been on a ship captured by HMS *Trent* it's almost certain she was an officer's servant; most freed slaves would have lived with the crew on the gun decks until they could be put ashore and Lindsay, as captain, would have had little contact with them. A higher ranked female servant like a personal secretary, however, would have got better treatment despite being a slave – perhaps a junior officer would even have been evicted from his cabin so she could move in there. It's also possible she would have been invited to dinner with the captain in his private cabin, as this was a reasonable social courtesy. That would have allowed a relationship to grow.

Attitudes to race in 18th century English society were complex. By modern standards the times were often appallingly racist, as the widespread aceptance and exploitation of slavery suggests. However the situation was actually a lot better than it would be a century later. Ideologies of racial superiority were only beginning to be developed and most apparently racist references were actually criticisms of cultures – it was common for anyone who wasn't English to be lumped together:

"The Indians, Black or Scotish (sic) Plotters

Cannot outvie these vile Bog-Trotters"

This 1735 anti-Irish rant compares the (white) Irish unfavorably with Indians, Africans and Scots.[xi] It's notable that the Scots, who are predominantly Anglo-Saxon and Celtic just like their southern neighbors, are classed together with non-Europeans from distant British colonies. These peoples weren't regarded as inferior because of the color of their skins; they were regarded as inferior because they weren't English. In 18th century England real xenophobic hatred was mostly directed at the (white) French.

However among the few non-whites in England were some freed slaves who had been educated by wealthy patrons, and they were a lot more socially acceptable than an Irishman (or even one of the English poor) would have been. It was only as colonies in the Americas began to rely heavily on slavery for economic development that modern-style racism became prevalent. In the 1760s it was possible for writer and composer Ignatius Sancho, born on a slave ship, to be an active member of London society and an anti-slavery activist.[xii] In fact Sancho, who supported himself by running a popular grocery store in between his various artistic ventures, was able to vote in British parliamentary elections – a privilege denied to 90 per cent of his white countrymen at the time. His anti-slavery letters were frequently published in the newspapers and widely discussed by politicians, and his friends included future prime minister Charles James Fox.

Of course many people's attitudes to men like Sancho were quite patronizing – they were seen as exotic, a sort of interesting novelty. Real social acceptance was limited, and it would have been unthinkable for any member of the upper classes to let their daughter marry one. In fact mixed-race children were not that uncommon in the British Empire (although rare in England itself) but they were mostly born to female slaves and certainly didn't belong to upper class society. If someone in John Lindsay's position fathered a child with a black woman the normal thing to do would be to pay off the mother and forget it had ever happened. If the mother was lucky the payment would be enough to support her and give the child some sort of education, and perhaps even set them up with a small business. Thomas Jefferson, who had six children with a mixed-race house slave, never acknowledged any responsibility for them but made sure they learned a trade; he later freed them in his will.

By the time he realized Maria was pregnant John Lindsay had probably earned enough in prize money to have given her a respectable payment and set her free on Jamaica or Antigua; it would have satisfied the social rules he lived by. Instead he chose a very different solution.

Chapter 4: The Infant And The Judge

We don't know exactly when Dido was born; equally we have no idea *where* she was born, either. The chances are, however, that it was in the captain's cabin of HMS *Trent*. This was a large room at the rear of the gun deck, around twenty feet long and stretching the full width of the ship. It was usually furnished with the captain's desk and chair, some bookcases and cabinets, a dining table with half a dozen seats and some sofas or armchairs so the captain could have conferences with his officers. Just forward of it was the sleeping cabin, a small compartment on one side of the ship where the captain would sleep in a hanging cot – a box-like bed suspended from the deck above. Usually he shared the compartment with one of the ship's guns, and there would be another on each side of the great cabin. All the walls between cabins were lightweight wood and canvas partitions, and when the ship went into action they were removed to leave the gun deck as a single open space. The walls and furniture would be stored below in the hold – if they were left on the gun deck and an enemy shot hit them they would be turned into a spray of lethal splinters. Most of the time the captain had some space to himself. If Maria gave birth on the frigate, as she almost certainly did, it would have been in Lindsay's sleeping cabin.

Women giving birth on one of the King's warships was hardly unheard of – in fact it was common enough that there was a piece of folk medicine attached to it. If the birth was difficult the captain would often fire a volley from the guns, in the belief that the shock of the recoil would hurry things along.[xiii] English author Jane Austen's brother Charles was a Royal Navy officer and, once he became captain of his own ship, routinely took his wife to sea with him. His fourth child was born in his cabin on the battleship HMS *Namur* in 1814, although sadly both mother and daughter died within a couple of weeks. Jane Austen wondered if her sister in law and niece might have survived if they'd come ashore shortly after the birth, but that's unlikely. Death in childbirth was extremely common at the time, and while a warship stank of stagnant bilgewater and the hundreds of men crammed into the hull it was still probably a healthier environment than a town. Apart from anything else it was free of the childhood diseases that killed so many infants.

For Maria there would have been another benefit to giving birth on HMS *Trent*. As a slave, had she given birth ashore she wouldn't have received any medical attention. A warship as large as a frigate carried a ship's surgeon, though, and as the captain's mistress she would have got the best medical care available at the time. In any case she gave birth to a healthy daughter. The infant was christened Dido Elizabeth Belle. Dido was perhaps a nod to her African ancestry; Dido was the legendary founder and first queen of the North African city of Carthage. It's not clear where Elizabeth came from, although it was a favorite in Lindsay's mother's family, and Belle seems to have been the surname Maria had adopted.

What happened to Maria next is unknown. Some versions of the story say she died not long after baby Dido was born, and unfortunately that's very likely. What's certain is that she wasn't around when the ship returned to Portsmouth in 1763. It's just possible that she refused to go to England and Lindsay put her ashore but insisted on keeping the baby, but sadly it's more probable that she died somewhere in the Caribbean or Atlantic and was buried at sea. That raises some questions about how Dido was cared for early in her life. Was Maria around long enough to feed her until she was weaned, or did Lindsay find another new mother on board who could act as a wet nurse? There was no real alternative to breastfeeding at the time; orphaned babies could be fed cow's milk in an emergency but that wasn't available on a warship. The crew lived on a tedious diet of salt beef, dried peas, hard-tack biscuits and cheese. The only nutritional supplements available were lime juice and rum. None of it was ideal for feeding a baby.

However he managed it, Lindsay brought Dido to England with him. He had to find a home for her, though. While he waited for a new ship he was on leave, but that wouldn't last long (in fact he took over another frigate, HMS *Tartar*, early in 1764 and by mid-May was back in the Caribbean). Lindsay was unmarried at the time and had no home where a child could be brought up. Luckily he found a solution in his extended family. His uncle, Lord Mansfield, was childless and happily agreed to bring up Dido.

William Murray, Baron Mansfield, was the younger brother of Lindsay's mother Amelia Murray. Born in 1705 at his prominent family's home in Perthshire, he was educated in Perth and London before going on to study at Christ Church College, Oxford. There he studied history, French and Latin. In 1727 he graduated and returned to London to train as a lawyer. Perhaps "train" is too strong a word. Legal education in England at the time was informal, to say the least. Potential barristers had to enroll at one of the four Inns of Court, which despite their name were professional societies. Those who performed well enough were called to the bar, but the required performance was not difficult – the pass grade was eating five dinners per term at the Inn and reading the first sentence of a letter handed over by the Inn steward. In practice the high membership fee was the main obstacle to candidates, and as a result the legal profession was dominated by the aristocracy.

After joining the bar in 1730 Mansfield quickly made a name for himself by being able to deal with the different legal systems operating in Britain. England and Scotland had unified in 1707 but each had kept its own law, and the conflicts between common law and Scots law could be confusing. Being Scottish himself, and having lawyers in the family – his brother David was a barrister in Edinburgh – he could resolve cases that involved both systems, and by the end of the 1730s he was one of the most prominent lawyers in London. One of the cases that made his name was the affair of Captain Porteous, an officer of the Edinburgh city guard who had been lynched after ordering his men to fire on a crowd. As punishment, Parliament wanted to disenfranchise the entire city; Mansfield persuaded them to reduce this to a fine.[xiv] He married Lady Elizabeth Finch in 1738 and became a Member of Parliament in 1742; by 1756 he was Lord Chief Justice, the head of the English judiciary.

Mansfield had a successful career and was happily married, but there was one thing missing in his life – children. He and his wife wanted children but none arrived. Then, sometime in late 1763, his nephew appeared with baby Dido. Lindsay had a request that was at the same time tempting and difficult; he wanted Mansfield and Elizabeth to bring up his daughter. It's obvious why that would have appealed to the couple – after years of hoping for a baby here was one being offered to them. Socially there could be pitfalls though. While they'd happily welcome the girl into their home there would be difficulties in getting her accepted by the aristocratic circles they moved in. The fact that she was mixed race would certainly be an issue, but in fact it was a comparatively minor problem. There was a much bigger one – Dido was illegitimate.

Today over 40 per cent of babies in the USA are born to unmarried mothers, and the percentage is similar in most European countries. For most people it's not a big deal. In the 18th century it was very different. Even among the poor illegitimacy carried a huge stigma, and for the upper classes it affected one of their key concerns – inheritance rights. If the Mansfields raised an illegitimate child it would cause no end of gossip in society and possibly the government. That must have been something they considered, but in the end their desire to have a child overcame any hesitation and they agreed to look after Dido.

Looking back from centuries later it's hard to appreciate just what a generous gesture that was. The Mansfields were wealthy, influential people, but they were happy to take in the daughter of a slave. It's been suggested that they accepted Dido as a playmate for her cousin Elizabeth, but examining the dates shows that's unlikely to be true. In any case Dido was soon installed with them at Kenwood House, their large home just outside London. Records from the local parish church for November 20, 1766 record the baptism of Dido Elizabeth, "Aged 5y". That suggests Dido was born before the Battle of Havana, although without an actual birth certificate it's not conclusive – records from the time aren't always reliable. But if Lindsay brought Dido to Kenwood in 1763 or 1764, why the delay in having her baptized? It's been speculated that Maria had survived the voyage to England and raised Dido herself until the age of five or so, but there's strong evidence that this isn't the case. Lord Mansfield had bought Kenwood House in 1754, and seems to have been happy with it. However it's known that when he and his wife made the decision to bring up children there they hired a well-known Scottish architect, Robert Adam, to remodel it into a more suitable home. Adam began work on the house in 1764.[xv]

In 1766 the Mansfields found themselves with a second girl to look after.[xvi] Lord Mansfield's nephew, Viscount Stormont, was the British ambassador to Vienna. He was married to Henrietta von Bünau, the widow of a German diplomat, and they had a daughter. Then in 1766 Lady Henrietta died suddenly. Even with his servants Stormont didn't feel he could bring her up himself in a foreign country, so he brought her to Kenwood and asked his uncle if he could care for her. Once again the Mansfields agreed. This time it was less of a dilemma, too; their great-niece, Lady Elizabeth Murray, was an aristocrat like themselves and was both white and legitimate. However she was also almost exactly the same age as Dido and the Mansfields seem to have realized that it would be good for both girls to bring them up together, almost as sisters. Perhaps, at that time, they decided it was time to have Dido baptized to formalize her status in the household. As the daughter of an unmarried slave she wouldn't have been baptized at birth but the patronage of England's top judge would have been able to get it done.

Now the Mansfields had two young girls at home; what would life have been like for Dido and Elizabeth? The most obvious fact about life at Kenwood is that it would have been extremely luxurious. The house wasn't as huge as it would eventually become but it was already large – there were at least 24 rooms with fireplaces. That would have included the kitchens, laundry and servants' quarters of course, but it's clear that Dido wasn't a servant. Very little is known about her early life but it's likely she and Elizabeth shared a governess, who would have acted as a combination nanny and tutor to them both. Most upper class children were home schooled at the time, but not by their parents; either a governess or when they were older a tutor would be employed to do it. It's clear that Dido did get an education, and it was rare for people to pay to educate their servants. As she grew older she also came to the notice of visitors to Kenwood. That's hardly surprising – with her coffee-colored skin she was an exotic and conspicuous member of what was otherwise a typical upper class household. What's more remarkable is her place within that household. Many of the nobility employed black servants but Dido was clearly something very different.

The Mansfields had many visitors, and some of these began to note Dido's presence. She didn't join them for meals as her cousin did, but after they had eaten and moved into the drawing room for coffee she would be there. For a servant to socialize with the family and their guests would have been completely unthinkable, so that alone makes clear that her status was much higher. Perhaps that was to be expected.

Lord Mansfield was a reactionary in some ways. He opposed increasing the freedom of the press, and was often criticized for his strong support of the king. That criticism came from both sides, because many English royalists claimed it was a cover for very different opinions. It's widely believed that he secretly supported the Jacobite movement, which his family had been involved in for decades. The Jacobites wanted to restore the Stuart dynasty to power in place of the Hanoverian kings who had ruled Britain since 1714. The Jacobites are often portrayed as a romantic movement trying to bring back a golden age of traditional British monarchy, but in fact their aims were alarming. As well as wanting to reduce the powers of the democratic parliament (which, at the time, didn't have all that many powers to start with) they planned to restore the Pope's authority over the British government – unlike the Anglican Hanoverians the Stuarts were Roman Catholic. They had some support in the Scottish Highlands and among many Catholics, but were generally unpopular in England and among Scotland's Protestant majority. However they were still dangerous; in 1745 a Scottish Jacobite army had invaded England and advanced to within 125 miles of London before retreating in the face of growing loyalist armies. The figurehead of the rebellion, "Prince" Charles Edward Stuart, was an egotistical fool but the actual army had been led by a very capable commander. His name was Lord George Murray, son of the chief of Clan Murray, and he was a distant relative of Lord Mansfield. That meant there was always a suspicion that he supported the Jacobites himself, even though he was a member of the British government during the 1745 uprising.

But in other ways Mansfield was known as a progressive. He was keen to reform England's ancient trade laws, originally developed in the Middle Ages, to make them more suitable for an industrial and trading nation. He made changes that speeded up court cases and made it easier for ordinary people to access the law. Then in 1772 he came face to face with the issue of slavery. By then Dido, who was legally a slave, had been living in his home for eight years.

Chapter 5: Somersett's Case

James Somersett was an African who'd been captured as a boy in 1749 and sold into slavery in the American colonies. His buyer was Charles Stewart, a Scottish-born merchant who had emigrated to Virginia and established a successful business there. Eventually he joined the customs service and by 1769 he had been promoted to Paymaster General of the American Customs Board. That year he returned to London to look after his widowed sister and he brought Somersett with him. Somersett was a favorite among Stewart's slaves; he had learned English quickly and well, and as he grew older Stewart began to use him as a personal secretary. For a slave Somersett was treated reasonably well and probably accepted his position in life. When he got to England, however, that began to change.

Somersett continued to help Stewart with his business affairs in England, but he had some free time as well and being articulate he soon started meeting people. Among his new acquaintances were both free blacks and abolitionists. By the time he'd been in London a year he had made many friends, had been baptized - collecting a number of English godparents in the process - and was thoroughly enjoying life in England. Whatever he'd thought back in America he now came to realize that slavery was unnatural and he was being exploited. In October 1771 he'd had enough and ran away from Stewart's house. Stewart wasn't willing to take the loss of his "property" lying down and put up wanted notices for the escaped man, and it worked; Somersett was recaptured the next month and brought back to his master.

Sometimes recaptured slaves were beaten and put back to work, but some owners preferred to punish this "disloyalty" by selling them into worse conditions. Somersett had been a favored slave; he'd been given good clothes, employed on light work and given a fair amount of freedom. Now Stewart sold him to the captain of a merchant ship about to sail for the West Indies. The captain, John Knowles, planned to sell Somersett to a sugar plantation when he reached Jamaica; for now he chained him up in the ship's hold.

It wasn't going to be that simple though. It wasn't technically illegal to keep a slave in manacles, because slavery wasn't actually forbidden by English law. Crucially it wasn't *permitted* by English law either, and now Mansfield received a petition from three London residents. One of them was Elizabeth Cade, who'd been at Somersett's baptism earlier that year. The petition they delivered was for a writ of *Habeus Corpus* – "You may have the body" – and it demanded that Somersett should be brought in front of an English court. In fact it had deeper, more significant implications too. A writ of *Habeus Corpus* was issued in the name of the king and its intention as to make sure nobody in Britain was denied due process of law. Charles Stewart might be a resident of Virginia but he was still a British subject, as was Knowles, and they couldn't defy the writ if Mansfield issued it. Their only hope of not having to produce Somersett in court would be if Mansfield ruled that the slave was property, not a person, and not entitled to that protection.

At first Mansfield's response wasn't encouraging. He tried to persuade both sides of the dispute to settle out of court. First he suggested that Cade should buy Somersett from Stewart and Knowles then give him his freedom. When she refused he applied pressure on Stewart to free Somersett himself (which would also have meant refunding Knowles the price he'd paid). Stewart didn't only refuse; he filed his own case accusing Somersett of having robbed him by running away. It seemed that both sides wanted their day in court, so Mansfield granted the *Habeus Corpus* writ. He ordered a hearing for January 24, 1772 and had Somersett released on bail (Cade paid it). He was going to have to hear the case, and whatever he decided was going to make law.

In fact that was the plan. As soon as Somersett was released he visited Granville Sharp, a clergyman's son and leading anti-slavery campaigner. Sharp had already been involved in several court cases brought by escaped slaves and he readily agreed to help Somersett. He felt it best not to be directly involved – he had crossed swords with Mansfield before and the Lord Chief Justice was not one of his admirers – but he had many contacts in the abolitionist movement and a good understanding of the law. Now he helped Somersett find lawyers to represent him (a public campaign raised enough money to pay his legal fees, although the lawyers insisted on working *pro bono*) and briefed them on the issues.

Sharp believed that this case was his best chance yet to strike a blow against the acceptance of slavery in England, and he wanted it to be as well prepared as possible. As a result Somersett's lawyers had to ask for more time, but Mansfield granted it and the case finally began on February 7. In total five lawyers argued for Somersett, including two holders of the elite Serjeant-at-law title, and they made several persuasive arguments. The first and probably most influential was that there was no law that established slavery as an institution. Laws in some colonies might permit it, they said, but colonial law was irrelevant in England and slavery had never been recognized by an act of parliament or by the common law. In fact common law dating back to the Magna Carta of 1215 stated that everyone had the right to liberty. It hadn't been perfectly applied but the principle was there.

Somersett's lawyers also brought up the subject of contract law. They reminded the court that English contract law did not allow anyone to enslave themselves, and that no contract was valid unless it was consented to by both parties. If a slave didn't consent to work for his master then, legally, he was not obliged to.

Stewart had his own lawyers with their own arguments. Their case rested on property rights; in their view Somersett was Stewart's property and couldn't be allowed to, in effect, steal himself. They also argued that there were dangers in freeing every slave in England – they estimated there were around 15,000 of them – at once. Mansfield was aware that the second argument did have some truth in it, but that was a minor point. The main thing about Stewart's arguments was that they would work on someone who viewed non-whites as objects rather than people. Stewart and his lawyers seemed to have forgotten – although it was being widely talked about – that when Mansfield left the court at night he went home to a black girl he was bringing up more or less as his own daughter.

One of the reforms Mansfield had made as Lord Chief Justice was to radically cut back on the practice of "reserved" judgments. Until he took the top job it had been normal practice for judges to hear a case then think it over at leisure, often calling the court back in months later to give their verdict. He felt that in most cases it was just laziness, or an excuse to bump up fees. This time, though, the issue was too complex – and too personal – for him to rule right away. Probably with great reluctance, he announced that he was reserving the case for a month. That's a sign of how much thought he was giving it, because the hearings had already taken over three months – the final one was on May 14.

We know from the diaries of visitors that Dido didn't eat meals with the Mansfields when there were guests at Kenwood, but what about the rest of the time? Did the judge discuss cases with her at home? It's fascinating to imagine what she would have made of James Somersett's situation. Her own origins went back to the same slave trade that had left Somersett in such an appalling position, but instead she had all the advantages of an upper class background – wealth, education and freedom. Perhaps she wondered what Somersett could have achieved given the same chances. Almost certainly she was revolted at the thought of a man being treated like a disobedient dog. It's unlikely that, aged ten, she would have dared give advice to her foster father. It's equally unlikely that when he returned to court on June 22 she was far from his mind.

When Mansfield finally delivered his judgment it was a complex and subtle one. He observed that a 1729 legal opinion had stated that slaves did not become free by being brought to England or undergoing baptism, and that owners had the right to return slaves from England to the colonies. This opinion clearly supported Stewart's case and Mansfield could have avoided any controversy by simply following it. He chose not to do so, and based his decision on what the laws of England actually said – or, in this case, didn't say. The key thing they didn't say was that it was permissible to own another human being as property.

Mansfield set the stage by making clear that nobody in England could be punished under a law that existed in another country, even if the person actually came from that country; what mattered in England was English law. He stated that the degree of power masters had over servants – and it's notable that he talked of servants, not slaves – was different in each country. That power, he said, must be regulated by the laws of the place where it was exercised, and Stewart was exercising power over Somersett in England. That was the key point, and it led to his conclusion: Nobody in England had ever been allowed to sell someone else abroad for refusing to serve them. He ended with a firm order – "The black must be discharged."

It's worth quoting Mansfield's conclusion in a bit more length, because as well as explaining why he ruled the way he did it gives some insight into what he was thinking as he did so:

The state of slavery is of such a nature, that it is incapable of now being introduced by Courts of Justice upon mere reasoning or inferences from any principles, natural or political; it must take its rise from positive law; the origin of it can in no country or age be traced back to any other source: immemorial usage preserves the memory of positive law long after all traces of the occasion; reason, authority, and time of its introduction are lost; and in a case so odious as the condition of slaves must be taken strictly, the power claimed by this return was never in use here; no master ever was allowed here to take a slave by force to be sold abroad because he had deserted from his service, or for any other reason whatever; we cannot say the cause set forth by this return is allowed or approved of by the laws of this kingdom, therefore the black must be discharged.

In this statement Mansfield rejected any idea that slavery could be justified by natural laws or political philosophy; stated that it could only be legal if explicitly permitted by law; said that no such law existed in England; and called the practice "odious". Despite its archaic legal language it was a clear and firm statement that English law did not justify slavery. If Dido had been in court to hear it she would have been proud.

Some modern commenters have actually criticized Mansfield for not going far enough; they believe he deliberately kept the ruling narrow – which in many ways he did – and that he should have explicitly stated that slavery did not exist in England. It's easy to sympathize with that view, given how appalling slavery actually was. Mansfield, however was worried about the consequences if he made such a ruling. It went without saying that it would be bad for the economy of the colonies, and even of England itself; if there were 15,000 slaves in England as Stewart's lawyers claimed, and their average price was £50 each, that would add up to around £750,000 in total. This is equivalent to about $140 billion in 2014 dollars, so it would have had a major impact on the economy. For the colonies it would have been disastrous, and there were political issues involved there. Mansfield was already unpopular with many people in the increasingly discontented American colonies – John Quincy Adams described him as "more responsible for the Revolution than any other man"[xvii] – and if he made a ruling that would have basically wiped out the lucrative sugar industry there would have been uproar. The colonists were increasingly rejecting the authority of London and moderates in the government were keen to calm the situation down. Mansfield was a member of the more hard line faction led by the king, but even so he knew that outlawing slavery would be an unbearable provocation.

Whatever 21st century legal experts feel about Mansfield's judgment, at the time it was seen as a great victory for the abolitionist cause. The public took the ruling to mean that slaves could not be held in England, and that widespread belief went a long way to making it a reality. The number of slaves in Britain fell sharply, and while English ports continued to be involved in the Atlantic trade the abolitionist movement continued to gain strength. There were cases where slave owners ignored Mansfield's ruling and shipped recaptured runaways to the West Indies but none of them tried to fight a case in court again. The verdict was also cited in several other cases involving slaves, and made its way into Scots law as well. In 1774 Joseph Knight asked his employer John Wedderburn to pay him a wage; when Wedderburn refused Knight ran away. Recaptured, he demanded a trial; after several conflicting verdicts and appeals the Court of Session, Scotland's highest court, supported Mansfield's decision and stated that slavery did not exist in Scotland. In 1807 British subjects were forbidden from owning slaves and the Royal Navy was ordered to start anti-slavery patrols off the African coast and in the Caribbean. Slavery was formally abolished throughout the British Empire in 1833. After the Somersett case the law had clearly turned against the practice and by the time the law officially changed it had mostly faded away from England.

Chapter 6: Life At Kenwood

Throughout the Somersett case lawyers, colonial slave owners and the public had been talking about Dido and how she might affect his attitude to the issue. That's not surprising; it must have occurred to Mansfield that by ruling against people being abducted to the colonies to be sold he might be protecting Dido herself. That must have weighed heavily with him. In general he was pro-business and in most ways supported the merchants whose trade between England and the colonies was doing so much to boost the country's prosperity, and by dealing such a heavy blow to the business of slavery he had endangered the economy of the West Indies colonies. He was also devoted to the law, though, and believed that it must be followed no matter what the consequences; "*fiat justitia, ruat coelum*", he said as he prepared to give judgment on Stewart and Somersett – "Let justice be done, though the heavens may fall".[xviii] With James Somersett a free man justice had certainly been done and the heavens had not yet fallen. Life in England went on.

How was that life for Dido, growing into a young woman at Kenwood? By the standards of the time it was extremely privileged. It's known that her bedroom – really a suite with a private dressing room and bathroom – was in the main quarters of the big house, not the servants' wing. Its luxurious furnishing makes it clear that by this stage she was very much one of the family. She also got an annual allowance of £30 and 10 shillings – more than $450,000 at current values. It was less than the £100 her cousin Elizabeth received but Elizabeth was heir to a title and was also the legitimate child of Mansfield's nephew. These two factors explain the difference; it's almost impossible that Dido's race played any part. After all if Mansfield had believed she was racially inferior her allowance would probably have been equivalent to a servant's wages, whereas in fact it was many times higher.

That's not to say that Dido didn't do anything to earn her allowance. Kenwood House wasn't a working farm but it did have its own small dairy and some poultry, to keep the kitchens supplied. Dido was responsible for running them. It's often thought that unmarried upper class ladies spent their entire lives socializing but in fact they usually played a major role in running their households, and Dido's tasks were quite typical. Her cousin almost certainly had her own jobs to do, perhaps assisting Lady Mansfield with the running of the house itself and managing the servants. Dido did have another job too, which was less usual; she helped Lord Mansfield with his correspondence, which would have been a busy job in itself – after all he was Britain's top judge. Normally men in his position employed a secretary to do this job, so it's unclear why Mansfield got Dido to do it. It does show that she was well educated, as otherwise he wouldn't have trusted her with such an important job. It also shows great faith in her discretion, because she would have been reading about high-level government business.

The business of the government nearly had serious consequences for her in 1780. Roman Catholics in Britain had faced official discrimination since the Popery Act of 1698; among other things it effectively made it illegal to be a Catholic priest. The law had been unevenly applied and by the mid-18th century it was unpopular with most educated people. Mansfield particularly disliked it and in 1778 he passed the Papists Act, which eliminated many (though not all) of the anti-Catholic laws. The intent behind the law was good; the timing could have been better. The American Revolutionary War was at its height and as well as the colonists Britain was fighting France, Spain and Holland. Various Protestant extremists began spreading rumors that Catholic officers in the army and navy were eager to join forces with the enemy (these rumors ignored the inconvenient fact that the Dutch were staunch Protestants) to reimpose absolute royal power (ignoring the even more inconvenient fact that the king was a Protestant...) and unrest began to grow. The disturbances coalesced around the Protestant Association of London, led by the eccentric Lord George Gordon.

On June 2, 1780 a large anti-Catholic crown marched on the Houses of Parliament. Lord Gordon presented a petition calling for the repeal of the Papists Act, which was legal, but his followers quickly became rowdy and tried to force their way into Parliament. Troops were called and dispersed the mob, but it then fanned out through the center of London. Chaos erupted and continued for the next two days. The embassies of Catholic countries were attacked, gangs rampaged through Irish immigrant areas and on the night of June 3 hundreds of rioters descended on Mansfield's London house. Lady Mansfield escaped with Elizabeth and Dido, just in front of the vicious mob; Mansfield wanted to stand his ground but was finally persuaded to leave by his manservant. The house was burned down and its valuable legal library – which contained the records of most of Mansfield's trials, including Somersett's case – was destroyed. Another mob of rioters attempted to destroy Kenwood House but were driven off by cavalry.

By the time the Gordon Riots were brought under control over 500 people had died. Another 30 of the rioters were convicted and hanged; Lord Gordon himself was charged with treason. At trial he was defended by his cousin, Lord Erskine, who argued that while Gordon had played a major role in the march that had started the riots he had not intended treason. Gordon probably believed that the defense was useless because the trial judge seemed likely to be biased – it was Lord Mansfield. Once again, though, he showed his dedication to justice and advised the jury that unless they were absolutely certain Gordon had planned treason their duty was to find him not guilty. That's exactly what they did. Mansfield would probably have preferred to see him hang – the destruction of his town house had cost him a fortune, as well as his priceless library – but he was too principled to allow it to happen.

Chapter 7: The Girl In The Picture

In the great hall of Scone Palace, Lord Mansfield's birthplace, hangs a striking painting that gives an excellent insight into Dido's status during her time at Kenwood. It's believed to have been painted sometime in the 1770s, probably by Johann Zoffany. The German-born Zoffany was one of the most popular painters in England in the late 18th century and produced many portraits of prominent people. This painting shows two teenaged girls in a garden. One, a white girl, is seated. Behind her is a colored girl, who at first seems to be walking past but on closer examination looks like she's about to sit down too. The girls are Lord Mansfield's adopted children, Dido and Elizabeth.

If there was any lingering thought that Mansfield might have treated Dido like a servant, the painting wipes it out. A servant would never have been featured so prominently in a family portrait, and in any case the girls are obviously friends. Elizabeth has one arm outstretched, her hand resting on Dido's arm, and they are both smiling at the artist. They're also both fashionably dressed, with Dido's outfit even having the edge on her cousin's. Elizabeth is wearing a dress with a constricting bodice and huge hooped skirt, while Dido has a much more flowing gown that looks like silk, as well as a stylish turban with a large feather in it. She also has one finger lightly placed against her cheek, as if she's drawing attention to the color of her skin.

In the painting the girls look to be around eighteen or nineteen. That was probably their happiest time at Kenwood, with Lord and Lady Mansfield as adoptive parents. Their narrow escape from the mob during the Gordon Riots seriously affected Lady Mansfield's health, though, and she never recovered; in 1784 she died. The next year Elizabeth married. That left Lord Mansfield and Dido alone at Kenwood – apart, of course, from dozens of servants. Mansfield himself was 80 years old by this time and his own health was failing. Knowing that he didn't have much longer to live he updated his will. His first draft gave Dido a bequest of £200, but he soon increased that to £500, plus an annuity that would give her an annual income of £100 for life. Aware that her position as the daughter of a slave was still precarious he also took care to note that she was a free woman.

As it turned out Mansfield lived for another eight years. In that time his trust in Dido seems to have been greater than ever; she now wrote letters on his behalf, often dealing with complex legal matters. They were joined at Kenwood by two middle-aged spinsters – both nieces of Mansfield's – the Ladies Anne and Margery Murray. This was a common arrangement for female relatives who hadn't married, and worked out well for everyone – Lady Anne seems to have taken over the running of the house, as she kept the account books from 1785 to 1793.[xix]

Dido's workload would have fallen in 1788, the year Lord Mansfield retired. Faced with claims that his abilities were fading he retired on June 4 that year. By coincidence, the same day Rear Admiral Sir John Lindsay died on his way home from a health cure in Bath. He was 51 years old but had been in poor health for several years, perhaps the legacy of a tropical fever. He was buried in Westminster Abbey, a traditional sign of honor. After his death his will revealed that he had either two or three illegitimate children. It's hard to be certain on this point; he left £1000 to a son and £1000 to a daughter, named as Elizabeth. This might have meant Dido but could also have been a second daughter, who some have identified as a Scottish woman named either Elizabeth Palmer or Elizabeth Lindsay. On the other hand an illegitimate daughter wouldn't have carried the Lindsay surname, so this may be a blind alley. It does seem unlikely that Sir John would have ignored Dido in his will after finding her a home with his uncle, who he was very fond of, but it's not impossible. There's no record of him having visited her during her life at Kenwood, although that doesn't prove much either way.

In any case Dido was now able to make her way in the world without any money from her father – when Lord Mansfield finally died in March 1793 she became a wealthy woman. Her £500 inheritance was more than enough to buy a house and the annuity gave her a generous income to live on. In fact many upper class women had less money available than Dido did. Of course she also faced disadvantages that women like her cousin didn't have to deal with; her skin was one, but her illegitimacy was a much larger one. That ruled out any chance of her marrying into the nobility. Lord Mansfield might have been happy to treat her as one of the family but the upper classes were very concerned with social status and having one of their sons marry a bastard would never have been permitted.

Dido couldn't marry into an aristocratic family, and in any case she was well past "marriageable" age – she was now in her early thirties. With Mansfield dead she couldn't stay at Kenwood either. Because Mansfield had no sons he had arranged for his title and the house to pass to David Murray, Lord Stormont. Elizabeth's father had remarried and had five children with his second wife, so it wouldn't be possible for Dido to remain in the house.

Chapter 8: The Rest Of The Story

Of course just because Dido couldn't marry the son of a wealthy, titled family didn't mean she couldn't make a respectable match. Sometime in the months after Mansfield's death she moved to the City of Westminster in central London. This was an affluent area, populated by the lower tiers of the aristocracy and wealthy merchants, and exactly where you would expect to find someone like Dido. Her exact address is unknown but church records show that she lived in the parish. They also show that on December 5, 1793 she married John Davinier, a gentleman's steward. Although Davinier was a servant, as a steward he was at the very highest level (senior to even a butler) and would have been in charge of all the other servants in the house. He would have been respectable, educated and well paid, and given Dido's strange social position the two would have been ideally suited. The marriage register shows that the couple was what would now be called upper middle class. The marriage was by license, which cost considerably more than marriage by banns and was common for society weddings. The church they chose – St. George's, Hanover Square – was a fashionable one; Theodore Roosevelt later married there. It's likely that the wedding was a major event, perhaps with aristocrats as guests.

Did Davinier continue to work after the marriage? With Dido's income he probably wouldn't have needed to, and between them they would have had a wide circle of social contacts. Sadly little is known about their married life beyond the fact they had three children; Charles and John, twins, were baptized in May 1795 and Thomas William in January 1802.

Unfortunately we can guess what happened next. In July 1804 Dido was buried at St. George's Fields, a cemetery belonging to the church where she had married Davinier. She would have been about 43 years old. Many women today have children at that age but modern medicine has made it much safer. In the first decade of the 19th century childbirth was dangerous and for a woman in her forties even more so. It's very possible that she died giving birth to her fourth child. If that's the case the lack of a baptism record makes it very unlikely the child survived.

Davinier remarried and had two more children, and also brought up the sons he'd had with Dido. John disappears from the records after his baptism and may have died as a child, but it's possible to find some details of Charles Davinier's life.[xx] He became an officer in the Indian Army, probably serving in the East India Company army first. It seems that his family made their careers throughout the British Empire; Dido's last known descendant, Harold Davinier, died childless in South Africa in 1975.

Conclusion

So what does the life of Dido Elizabeth Belle say to us today? Her origins are an eloquent condemnation of the evils of slavery; her mother had been forcibly removed from her home in Africa and taken to the Caribbean to be exploited. She was among millions of people whose lives were dislocated over a period of centuries, in a trade that took decades of military pressure to suppress and that still occasionally bubbles up around the African continent today.

There are also some more positive aspects, though. John Lindsay, however he met Dido's mother, had enough affection for his daughter to place her in the best hands he could think of. Lord Mansfield seems to have shown no consideration for her skin color and gave her every advantage in life he could arrange – during her life at Kenwood she was without doubt part of England's social elite, and after his death he left her wealthy in her own right. Perhaps having her in his family circle sharpened his own opposition to slavery and shaped his judgment in the Somersett case, which became one of the defining moments of the abolitionist movement in Britain.

When Dido left Kenwood she was able to find a husband and raise a family in a good area of London. Of course her life was very different from that of most of London's small black community – she was rich and free, where most of them were poor or enslaved. Perhaps some of them resented her, but perhaps others saw her as a symbol of hope, a sign that one day freedom and opportunity in England wouldn't depend on the color of your skin. It took too long, but that day finally came. Dido would have been pleased to see it.

Like many people's at the time- especially women – Dido's life was cut short far too early. All that remains today is the iconic portrait of her and her cousin, and some fragmented references to her in diaries and official records. It's still possible to piece them together though, and the picture that emerges from these puzzle pieces is an extraordinary one of tolerance and compassion in a harsher, more brutal age. It's a story that can – and should – inspire everyone.

Bibliography

[i] Tunstall, Brian (1990), *Naval Warfare in the Age of Sail*

[ii] Nuevo Mundo, *Reading the 1762 British occupation of the city*
http://nuevomundo.revues.org/61119

[iii] UC Berkeley Center for Latin American Studies, *Slavery and the Siege of Havana,* Raphael Murillo
http://clas.berkeley.edu/research/cuba-slavery-and-siege-havana

[iv] Allen J. Frantzen and Douglas Moffat, eds. *The Work of Work: Servitude, Slavery, and Labor in Medieval England* (1994)

[v] University of Illinois at Chicago, *European Disease In The New World*
http://www.uic.edu/classes/osci/osci590/3_3%20European%20Disease%20in%20the%20New%20World.htm

[vi] Mtubani, V.C.D, *African Slaves and English Law*

http://archive.lib.msu.edu/DMC/African%20Journals/pdfs/PULA/pula003002/pula003002007.pdf

[vii] Oxford Dictionary of National Biography, *Sir John Lindsay*

[viii] Byrne, Paula (2014), *Belle: The True Story of Dido Elizabeth Belle*

[ix] Byrne, Paula (2014), *Belle: The True Story of Dido Elizabeth Belle*

[x] BBC History, *Women in Nelson's Navy*

http://www.bbc.co.uk/history/british/empire_seapower/women_nelson_navy_01.shtml

[xi] Hunt, Margaret, *Racism, Imperialism and the Traveler's Gaze in Eighteenth-Century England*
http://www.academicroom.com/article/racism-imperialism-and-travelers-gaze-eighteenth-century-england

[xii] Gerzina, Gretchen (1995), *Black London: Life Before Emancipation*
[xiii] Mariner's Museum, *Women and the British Navy*

http://www.marinersmuseum.org/sites/micro/women/goingto sea/navy.htm
[xiv] Oldham, James (2004), *Common Law in the Age of Mansfield*
[xv] English Heritage, *Kenwood House*
   http://www.english-heritage.org.uk/daysout/properties/kenwood/history-and-research/kenwood-history-portico/
[xvi] Heward, Edmund (1979), *Lord Mansfield*
[xvii] Waterman, Julian S. (1934), *Mansfield and Blackstone's Commentaries*
[xviii] Chicago-Kent Law Review (December 1994), *Let justice be done, though the heavens may fall*

http://scholarship.kentlaw.iit.edu/cgi/viewcontent.cgi?article=2966
[xix] Byrne, Paula (2014), *Belle: The True Story of Dido Elizabeth Belle*
[xx] BBC Home, *Inside Out: Abolition of the British Slave Trade special*

http://www.bbc.co.uk/london/content/articles/2007/02/27/insideout_abolition_special_feature.shtml

Made in the USA
Lexington, KY
02 July 2014